LARRY COLEMAN

FISHERMEN & HOOKERS

ISBN-10: 1478378603

ISBN-13: 9781478378600

Library of Congress Control Number: 2012914464

CreateSpace Independent Publishing Platform

North Charleston, South Carolina

DEDICATION

I wrote this work in order to help people understand how they are being influenced by a small group of people with huge amounts of money. These few wealthy people are convincing voters to cast their precious votes in ways that are not in the voter's best interest. For more than two and a quarter centuries, patriots have fought and paid with their blood for this right to vote. None of us should take this right for granted. I am dedicating this work to the brave men and women who have served, are serving, and will serve this the greatest of all countries. I toured the national cemetery in Holly, Michigan, and it is not yet full of these patriots. Hopefully, it never will be. These patriots who served in order that we may be free to vote should be remembered when we exercise that right. The ones who made the ultimate sacrifice are standing in the booth with you. Some of the ones that made it home after their service may, in fact, be voting in the booths next to you. We should honor the ones who served and are still with us, as well. Thank a veteran when you can. It would be a wonderful thing to not need these patriots. Maybe one day we can achieve a world without war. Until that day comes, I hope you honor these patriots and their service and sacrifice by spreading the truth when you can. I ask that you take it upon yourself to find out what the truth is. Please don't accept some pundit's words or an advertisement paid for by a patriotic-sounding political action committee as the truth. Find out who puts the money into the political action committee and why. If the answers lead you to representatives who you think will not act in your best interests, then you must find representatives who will. The saying that "nothing is free" is very true about casting a vote. Your right to vote has been paid for dearly in time, in service, and in the blood of patriots. I hope to share nothing but the truth with these words. I will express my opinions here, but I also hope you will find that my opinions are based on facts and the truth. The truth is that which we are always trying to find and we must try to get the truth to the people who need it. Sometimes the truth is not the easiest thing to find. I feel your service, in seeking the truth and making it known, is deserving of those to whom I am dedicating this work. I think of voting as our "bloodstained right." I do not use this description lightly. I feel that voting may be the most precious right guaranteed in our Constitution. Please, seek the truth and use it when you vote.

FOREWORD

This work is a simple analogy to show how big money is influencing our politics in the United States today. I forced myself to keep this as short and simple as possible. I would like it to be read by as many people as possible, even by those who don't normally have or take the time to read. It is a simple, easy read. I hope you enjoy it, understand it, and take action to further inform yourself and others because of this work. It is important because our democracy is at a crossroads. There are a few wealthy people on the far right wing of our politics that would very much like to do away with our democracy and rule over us like kings. They have been and are financially supporting and putting in place political figures that are akin to the knights of days gone by. These politicians support and fight for these wealthy few who provide them with the money they need to stay in office. In this work, I call the people with the wealth and most of the real power "fishermen." I call their political figures "hookers." The wealthy have bought these political hookers (or at least rented them until their terms are over) through payoffs, campaign donations, and other gifts. The wealthy fishermen expect to get exactly what they want from their political hookers. These things usually take the form of legislation made to sound as good as homemade apple pie to the general public but in fact these pieces of legislation are being put in place for the benefit of the fishermen. As much as anything else, I hope you will realize that our elected officials are losing, if they haven't already lost, most of the power to control our government. The power is edging toward the hands of some of the wealthiest people in the world. It will be a very bad thing for the rest of us if this happens completely. Don't take my word for it, though. Research and investigate what is said in political communications and find out why it is being said. If you can, follow the money. In the recent Supreme Court decision in the Citizens United v. Federal Election Commission case the Court said basically that the First Amendment to the Constitution prohibits the government from restricting political expenditures by corporations. This 5-4 decision split along party lines and favoring the right wing of the court gives corporations the right to spend unlimited amounts of corporate funds for campaign advertising. Because of this very controversial decision there are now vast practically unlimited amounts of virtually untraceable money from both domestic and foreign corporations flowing into The United States' political process. Because of this decision, following the money is becoming nearly impossible. That decision must be overturned as soon as possible for the sake of our freedom and democracy. Do your best to get the truth. Use *all* sources available. Find the truth. Take action and vote.

TABLE OF CONTENTS

FISHERMEN

In the real world, fishermen try to catch fish. Most recreational fishermen use a fishing pole with a line tied to a baited hook. The hook is concealed in the bait and that hook is used to catch the fish. The fish don't see the hook. They don't know the hook is there. But the fish do see the bait. The bait looks like food to them and they are fooled into trying to eat it. More often than not, if the fisherman has done his job, a fish falls for the trick and is hooked.

There are some people in the world who have enough money to do almost anything they want to do. They can even have laws put in place, ended, or changed. If a law does not suit their specific needs, they use their wealth to change the law. They have even gone so far as to change laws that involve homicide. These are the so-called stand your ground laws that have allowed a man to shoot and kill an unarmed minor in the minor's own neighborhood. These laws were then used to allow the shooter, after basic questioning, to be set free. It was only after a national outcry for his arrest and trial that the shooter was even arrested. The people who have the money to get these sorts of laws passed are the "fishermen" in this work. It is difficult to say exactly how many of these fishermen there are. Most of them choose to live in the shadows that their wealth can easily provide. What qualifies them as fishermen? They usually are worth at least a billion dollars or more. They want and are willing to pay for laws to be passed that will benefit them. They really couldn't care less if regular people suffer or even die because of these laws. They just want theirs and are willing and able to spend whatever it takes to get what they want.

The fishermen in this work are like the fishermen in the real world in many ways. In the real world, a fisherman has two advantages over fish: intelligence and power. Fishermen, in this work, also have these two advantages. Our fishermen usually have the advantage of more education than the "fish" (voters) they are trying to catch. As far as power goes, our fishermen have at their disposal huge almost limitless amounts of money through which they have immense power.

The word "millionaire" has pretty much lost its punch in today's world. Millionaire used to mean that you had some power. In today's world however, the word millionaire or even multi-millionaire only means that you are quite well off. Mitt Romney, the presumptive Republican presidential nominee at the time of this writing, is, for example, a multi-millionaire. His worth has been estimated to be in the $250 million range. But even he is not the kind of "wealthy" I am discussing in this work. The wealthy I refer to as fishermen in this work are many of the richest four hundred people in the world. The people we are discussing usually have some type of citizenship in the United States but that is merely a formality that allows them to fish in the United States' political world. These fishermen have many multiples of the wealth that Mitt Romney has. Two examples of this type of fisherman are the Koch brothers. David and Charles Koch, who inherited a petrochemical business and fortune, are two of our fishermen whose combined wealth has been estimated at somewhere near $100 *billion*. Another is casino magnate Sheldon Adelson, whose wealth is in the $25 billion range. Donald Trump might be included in the list of fishermen, though some disagree about the size of his wealth. There are many more. It would only take one, but when there are dozens, perhaps, even hundreds, their political influence become almost insurmountable. These fishermen all have agendas that are often very similar. They want fewer taxes and less regulation. This is like bank robbers saying they want fewer, if any, policemen and no security systems in banks.

It is critical for us to get a grasp on how much money just these two very politically active Koch brothers have. They are only two of the several hundred on the right who have and are willing to use massive amounts of money to influence, if not completely change, the outcomes of our elections and thereby the very course of our government. Now, let me try to put in perspective how much money we are dealing with when we speak of fishermen.

A billion dollars is a truly staggering amount of wealth. A billion dollars is one thousand million. It is $1,000,000,000.00. Did you find yourself counting zeros? Scientific calculators go into scientific notation to display the numbers in a billion because they often don't have enough columns for that many digits. Think of the largest lottery game that has ever been won. It was in the Mitt Romney wealth range. If, for instance, you had $250 million (Mitt Romney's estimated personal worth) in $100,000 bills and packaged them in bundles of fifty. Each bundle would contain $5 million and be would be about one-half inch thick. The entire amount would be around two feet tall. A billion dollars would stack four times that height, or around the height of an average ceiling.

The Koch brothers are worth about $50 billion each. Individually, their stacks would be around four hundred feet tall, or about as high as a forty story building. Between the two of them, their stack of bundled $100,000 bills would be eight hundred feet tall.

Another way to get a grasp of this type of wealth would be to bundle $1 bills in bundles of one hundred. At about three-quarters of an inch per bundle, it would take 128 of these bundles to reach from the floor to a standard eight-foot-tall ceiling. The United States dollar bill is a little over six inches long and around two-and-a-half inches wide. With these bundles we could fill a 2,050 square foot house floor to ceiling, wall to wall, with Mitt Romney's money. But it would take four of these houses for a billion dollars. It would take a subdivision of four hundred of these houses to hold the Koch brothers' staggering $100 billion. It has been estimated that the combined spending by this group of billionaires (our fishermen) was at least four of these houses of money in the 2012 election just to make sure that President Barack Obama is not reelected. But please don't be worried for them. Even after spending that staggering amount, they will still have the equivalent of subdivisions of houses full of money.

There is one more thing you will want to keep in mind while reading this work. The fact is that there are hundreds of these right-leaning multi-billionaires who are heavily, and quite secretly, involved in both United States and world politics. Not all billionaires favor right or far-right politics. Almost invariably when discussing the topic of billionaires supporting the right wing, those on the right bring up George Soros as being a billionaire that supports progressive liberal causes. He does in fact support progressive liberal causes but he has no hidden agenda. Of the billionaires who are involved in politics, though, the vast majority promotes, favor and support right and far-right ideas and politicians. The reasons why the majority of billionaires lean politically to the right are clear if one looks closely. They are in the process of putting in place people who will pass legislation that will make it far easier to maintain and grow their already huge fortunes. Other extremely important legislation supported by and for the fishermen will also allow them to pass those amassed fortunes on to their heirs with little or no taxes. Politicians on the right are often heard saying, "Less government and less taxes for the job creators." This is right wing code for less regulation and more on the bottom line for multi-billionaires. These fishermen are typically unelected, extremely wealthy men and women who are using their wealth and power to influence the minds of our citizens. This influence is most often used to get citizens to vote for right or far-right politicians and also right-favored proposals that are beneficial to the fishermen, but won't be as good for the citizens casting their votes. In fact, proposals passed and people elected are often quite harmful to these citizen voters.

To be clear, the fishermen are the mega rich. But we must realize that they are personally not the ones trying to catch the fish. Our fishermen are the ones who make it possible for the politicians to get enough votes to be elected. In this work, the word "fish" refers to the hearts, minds, and *votes* of the voters in the United States. The baits are the ideas that fishermen present, through their paid for politicians, to the voters in order to win their votes. Like the fish in the water, these ideas, or baits get them to bite and thereby to be hooked. Hopefully this work will get people to question and investigate these ideas much more closely. If nothing else, I hope this will inspire people to follow the money. The recent Citizens United Supreme Court decision makes following the money nearly impossible. As has been said again and again, "Things that are worth doing are often not easy." Our fishermen are relying on this fact. Perhaps, if we all do our due diligence, we can catch the fishermen before they catch us.

HOOKERS

In the real world, fishermen bait their hooks and wait until they think they have a fish on the line, and then they pull firmly on the pole to tighten it. This is called "setting the hook." The action pulls the hook through the bait and snags the fish. Sometimes the hook is set in the fish's mouth. This is a good thing for the fish, since fishermen sometimes practice catch and release. Other times, the fishermen let the fish swim or run with the bait for a period of time. This running allows the fish to swallow the bait. When a fish swallows the bait before the fisherman sets the hook, it catches in the fish's throat or gills. This is almost always fatal for the fish.

Who are the hookers? The hookers are the politicians paid to pull in the fish (votes). Hookers are the politicians that have been bought by the fishermen to do what the fishermen need done. Many people think the politicians are the ones with the power. The hookers are merely the politicians that the voting public sees as the ones with power. The fishermen drive the boat. These fishermen, though, are rarely seen with or even close to the hookers, since that could be a bad thing for them both. The hookers just pull in the fish and do with the fish (that is, the power derived from their votes) what the fishermen want done.

The hookers are told by the fishermen the course for the boat. The fishermen tell their paid deckhands, including the hookers, what kind of fish they want to catch. The hookers are told by the fishermen the time and place to fish and the type of bait that is going to be used. The fishermen tell the hookers how and when to set the hook.

With this concept in mind we need to consider the difference between leaders and those that lead? They are very closely related, but they are definitely not the same thing. Leaders are people who are given the consensus opinion of their constituency. Leaders are elected to represent this consensus in order to pass laws that will benefit the majority of their constituency. Not everyone is completely satisfied, but the majority view is represented. This is the essence of democracy. Some call it government by the governed.

On the other hand, there are those who lead. They start out with an idea. Those that lead do what they can to persuade others that their ideas are good ideas. This might be called democracy, but it is, in fact, just good salesmanship. This work is about those who lead and the ways that they get their ideas put into effect through legislation. Those who lead are not part of a democracy; they are part of an oligarchy or plutocracy.

Why is it necessary for some to be leaders and others to lead? The answer is in simple numbers. There are those who have the immense wealth and could easily become one of our fishermen but choose instead to be leaders. Then there are those with immense wealth who only want to represent their own personal interest. They have ideas about how our country should be governed that will greatly benefit themselves. They want laws and the way we are governed to be changed to benefit their interest, but not the interest of the majority of our citizens. We live in a democracy, which means that no matter how much wealth a citizen has, each citizen has one and only one vote. Therefore, in a democracy, if you have an idea that will benefit you or you and just a few of your rich friends, you must lead others to *believe* that your ideas will help people enough so that they will cast their votes in favor of your ideas, or the person or persons who will legislate for your ideas.

It is similar to the discussion about whether our economy will grow more by giving the so called "job creators" tax breaks or by giving the average person a bigger share of the national wealth. On the one hand, some people have been led to believe that job creators will invest their tax savings in job creation. They may eventually hire workers but only if and when they absolutely can't do it any other way. On the other hand, it is proven fact of economics that sharing more of our national wealth with average people will enable and encourage those people to go out and spend money on goods and services, which will in fact create the need for more production and workers.

THE USS MISS INFORMATION

Every real-life fisherman needs to be able to get his hook out to where the fish are. Some fishermen do their fishing from the shoreline. Some fish from bridges, docks, and piers. Still other fishermen wade out in the water and cast into the surf. The fishermen who plan to catch the most fish use boats. Boats enable fishermen to go out in deep water where the large schools of fish live. Some fishermen have little row boats. Others fishermen have bigger boats with small motors. The boats get larger and larger, to the point of huge commercial fishing vessels with captains and deckhands. These deckhands are people who specialize in everything from setting the hooks to baiting the lines.

The boat that our fishermen use to get out into the water of the American political arena is intended to eventually hook huge groups of fish.

Many people who own boats like to name them and the names are often preceded by the word *Miss*. They might be called the *Miss Budweiser*, the *Miss Conception*, or the *Miss* whatever. The names express the thinking of the owner of the boat. I thought a long time about the name of our fishermen's boat. I thought I might call her the *Miss Constitution*, as the right wing is often heard misinterpreting the Constitution to make some obscure right wing political argument. But, that is not how our fishermen get to the deep water where the fish are. I thought about naming their boat the *Miss ALEC*. ALEC is the acronym for the American Legislative Exchange Council, which is a right wing lobbying organization that previews and approves all proposed right wing legislation. That was a good name, but not quite right for the fishermen's boat. Then, on my morning walk, I was thinking about a reply I had written to an online news article about the George W. Bush administration of misinformation. That was it. It seems to me that what our fishermen are doing is using their wealth and power to misinform people for the purpose of basically stealing their votes. This indoctrination by the use of misinformation is what I write about almost daily. This misinformation that is comprised of half-true, stretched, bent, or broken facts is what the fishermen use to influence people. Therefore, I christen our fishermen's boat the USS *Miss Information.*

This name exactly describes the right wing policies of misinformation. They are using words and phrases that sound very patriotic and true, but if one looks a little deeper into the phrases and catch lines, the real meaning is there but very well hidden. Phrases like "less government" sounds good to many of the fish that our fishermen are trying to catch. Sadly, and much too often, these phrases do catch many voters. In reality, the "less government" phrase means less regulation for all kinds of the *fishermen's* commercial activities. Less government will mean less environmental protection. It means the quality of our water, air, food, and all of the things that we come in contact with in our daily lives will surely be diminished in safety and quality. It means the products and services that we, as consumers, buy and use will take major hits as far as the standards by which they are made. The methods and materials used to manufacture them will also be diminished. These words and phrases are used by our fishermen through their hookers and crew to sound like one thing to the general public, but in the world of our fishermen they mean something completely different.

UNION BOATS

Commercial fishing, as most of us have seen on television, is called the most dangerous job. It really does not have to be that dangerous. The problem is that the fishermen and the crew are paid by the number of pounds of fish that are caught. With this type of incentive pay, a factor of greed comes into play. Whenever greed comes into a work situation, safety can be pushed aside. Safety is replaced by greed and expediency often with devastating consequences.

First of all, let me say that I am and will always be very pro-labor. By that I mean organized or unionized labor. I am not naïve enough to believe that unions are perfect entities. I understand that some people feel unions have become too powerful. Some believe that unions help workers who are lazy and not so much those who really want to work. I have heard right wing pundits argue at length that the union dues paid are not worth the representation provided and that the government should not "force" people to pay union dues. People are free not to pay these union dues. All they have to do is find another place to work that does not have a union. Should the government be able to make us pay for the things we get at the grocery store? It is the same thing, except that union represented workers are paying for a service their union provides. People have been led to believe that all union workers are overpaid and underworked. Some of these beliefs *may* be at least partially true. Sometimes unions do negotiate for those who are less likely to be good workers and for the right of the less ambitious worker to get a chance at redemption instead of discharge. But this is done in conjunction with the companies' desire to negotiate away other minor issues that might cost the company money.

I worked for almost ten years in a retail chain represented by what was then called the Retail Clerks Union Local 40. I have also worked in two United Auto Workers' represented automobile factories. One union was UAW Local 581 in Flint, Michigan, which represented the workers in the General Motors Corporation, Fisher Body Plant. I was also a proud member of the UAW Local 7, which represents the assembly workers in Chrysler Corporation's Jefferson North Assembly Plant (JNAP) in Detroit, Michigan. I also worked for ten years in nonunion auto parts manufacturing in Michigan. Take it from one who has been in both worlds; the union-represented work environment is right off the top, far safer. That alone is worth the union dues paid. In addition to the safety issues are the union-negotiated pay and benefits. The fishermen also say that union labor drives up the cost of the products they produce. The fact is that businesses often run up the price of their products and then use labor as a reason for doing so. The fact is that when a labor union negotiates a wage increase, the company invariably cuts an appropriate number of employees to more than pay for the increase in labor cost caused by the newly negotiated wage increase. The fishermen, at the same time that they are cutting labor to cover the increasing labor cost will also raise the price of its products to cover the cost of the labor increase. So the fact is that the companies benefit at both ends by cutting the number of laborers and increasing the prices of their products.

Labor unions in the United States were formed when our industries were booming. Workers saw those at the top becoming wealthier, while the workers' lives stayed about the same—terrible. After the Great

Depression, it was thought for a long time that if you had a job, you had better be glad about it no matter how low the pay or how awful the working conditions. The company bosses would work their employees without any concern for the workers' health or welfare. At the same time, wages were stagnant while corporate profits *soared*. These things needed to be addressed and the only way to do that was through organization and unionization. Everything in the arsenal of business foul play was used to keep unions out of major industries. This foul play included late night visits to employees' homes by armed thugs hired by companies to threaten and intimidate workers and their families about joining or even talking about unions. Eventually, though, through much struggle and even bloodshed, unions eventually prevailed. After unions were "allowed" several very good things began to happen, the biggest of which was better wealth distribution. Those at the top continued to get wealthy, but those at the bottom started to get a fairer share of the wealth generated by their labor. In addition to this was the fact that the safety of American industry began to rapidly improve. As with any organization, there might be some problems that labor unions need to address, but these two things, safety and fairer wealth distribution are so very important that the other things pale by comparison. That is, unless you are a fisherman.

In addition to the USS *Miss Information*, there are other boats out fishing in our political waters of the United States of America. These boats are labor unions. We will call them "union boats." There are many of them, but they are far smaller boats compared to the huge vessel of the fishermen. These union boats have far less fishing line (money) than do the fishermen. Though there may be more of these union boats because they are much smaller in size, they cannot compete with the larger, more powerful boat of the fishermen. The union boats are not allowed to go into the deep waters of bent fact and distorted truth in which the USS *Miss Information* thrives. Because of this lack of money, union boats just can't put out as much bait (political advertising) or fish for as long a time as the fishermen. Our fishermen are also aware that the majority of the fish really like the bait that the union boats are using. This better bait is interfering with the fishermen's plan to destroy the unions and then take control of our government. Consequently, the fishermen are doing everything they can to sink the union boats. The fishermen have, through the use of very effective baiting, even brainwashed some members of labor unions to support the right wing and even right-to-work legislation. This is like convincing fishermen to drill holes in the bottom of the boat while they are at sea. Now is that democracy? I think not. It is just good salesmanship and misinformation. My opinion is that it's probably a lot of both.

One of our fishermen's favorite baits is telling people how bad labor unions are for business. Our fishermen use this bait even though the facts are that the higher wage and benefit packages negotiated by and for the members of labor unions encourage the growth of our economy through those higher wages and benefits. In areas where labor unions are more prevalent, you will see more hospitals, shopping malls, restaurants, theaters, and other places where money is spent and jobs are created. These higher-wage union jobs create more jobs in the communities in which they are located. Usually these newly created businesses are places that younger people can get jobs and start their careers. People in these communities might even open a small business where it can grow and thrive.

There are several union boats trying to catch the same fish that the USS *Miss Information* is trying to catch, including the National Education Association, *Miss NEA*; United Auto Workers, *Miss UAW*; United Mine Workers,

*Miss UMW; Miss Teamsters; Miss Firefight-
ers;* Association of Federal Municipal City
Employees, *Miss AFMCE,* and others. They
are all out on the lake of public opinion trying to compete with the fishermen. The fishermen do not like the competition from the
union boats. The fishermen are willing to do
any dirty trick they can think of to end the
competition created by our union boats. The
fishermen know that if they use their huge
boat, the USS *Misinformation,* they can surely
severely damage or destroy union boats in the
United States. The fishermen's plan is and has
always been to severely damage and, if possible, destroy the union boats. The fishermen
are doing everything they can, including lying
and worse, to rid themselves of the union
boats. If they can destroy the union boats, the
fishermen will have won, for theirs will be the
only large voice left in American politics. If
that day comes, it will indeed be a bad, bad
day for our democracy.

BAITS

In the real world, fishermen use baits to deceive fish. The fish are fooled into thinking that the bait they see is food. The bait looks and may even smell like food to the fish. Sometimes it may even be the food that the fish might normally see and eat. It might be a worm or a minnow. But the difference is that a fisherman's bait always has a hook hidden in it. Sometimes the bait is an artificial lure made from wood or plastic or other deceptive material. It might be shiny to reflect sunlight in murky water. The bait might wiggle and vibrate to simulate an injured or dying fish or bug. But there is always a well-hidden hook in the fisherman's bait.

So it is with our fishermen. They present "baits" to the fish through their bought-and-paid-for politicians, or hookers, who fool them into believing that the bait is going to be good for them. The hookers might say, for instance, that giving tax breaks to people like our fishermen will create jobs. This bait has worked very well and has hooked many fish for our fishermen. It is one of the baits that have hooked many of the biggest of the small fish in our lake. These bigger of the small fish are the voters in the upper middle class. They feel that they work hard and deserve a tax break. What this bait doesn't convey to these upper middle class fish is that these tax cuts once in place will no longer be able to be used for the things that the middle class will need to make their world a better place. Things like schools, teachers, roads, hospitals, police, and firemen are what these tax cuts will cut back, if not eliminate from their world. The fishermen bait these upper middle class fish with food that the fishermen themselves would eat: tax breaks. In North Carolina, real fishermen use shrimp to catch catfish. The shrimp are tiny and abundant, and the catfish are huge and tasty. What this translates to is that a small percentage tax break to a middle class or even upper middle class person might be a couple of thousand dollars at the maximum. The same small percentage tax break for a fisherman billionaire will amount to much more. It may even be in the millions of dollars. Also, in the same tax cut bills are deductions for things that the average middle or upper middle class person more than likely won't be able to use. Our fishermen, on the other hand, can and very much do use these tax advantages to their benefit.

Another of the baits that our fishermen use is the gun control issue. Our fishermen, with the help of the National Rifle Association (NRA), have baited and hooked a huge school of fish with this single issue. With lots of money and advertising, the NRA has led people to believe that they will have their guns taken away from them if they vote for anyone other than NRA-backed candidates. In the winter of 2011 and into 2012, the people of Wisconsin tried to recall Republican Governor Scott Walker. The NRA poured a massive amount of money into the election to say that the Democrat running in opposition to Walker, former Milwaukee Mayor Tom Barrett, was an anti-gun person (which he is not) and that if he were elected governor, he would take away hunters' deer rifles. This was blatantly false. The opposite was more likely. Governor Walker, whom the NRA supported, already had a plan to make a Texas pay-to-hunt rancher the Wisconsin hunting czar. This czar plans to turn vast tracts of land in Wisconsin, both public and private, into pay-to-hunt ranges. These people will not take away your guns but they will make it far more difficult and expensive to hunt in Wisconsin. So the NRA will continue to make money from memberships, as will the pay-to-hunt ranchers. Some of these pay-to-hunt ranchers are our fishermen. This group of fishermen will profit from gun and ammunition sales as well as the planned pay-to-hunt ranges.

Much of the NRA gun issue is parallel to the next bait, which is fear. This bait has caught, and will continue to catch, massive groups of fish. Along with the NRA's campaign to make gun owners believe that the left side of our government wants to take away your hand-guns, deer rifles, and shotguns, our fishermen are pushing a campaign of fear. For decades the American people were indoctrinated to believe that the communists were coming. They were going to take away everything we have and then torture us. They would then work us to death in forced labor camps. This campaign of fear suddenly shifted after the fall of the Soviet Union and became a cam-paign of fear of Muslims. The fishermen need this fear as bait to make us believe in the need to keep a huge military/defense budget in place. If there were nothing to fear, there would be no need for the United States to spend as much on our defense as the next twelve highest spending nations in the world combined spend on theirs. These nations are Germany, United Kingdom, France, Canada, Saudi Arabia, Australia, Japan, China, Turkey, Italy, Brazil, South Korea, India, and Russia. Because of what nineteen terrorists did on September 11, 2001, and at an estimated cost of less the $500,000, we have spent several trillion dollars, tens of thousands of American lives, and hundreds of thousands of the lives of other countries' citizens. Fear keeps the money flowing to defense contractors. Many of the owners of these defense contractors and their board members are, in fact, some of the fishermen.

This fear bait is also used by hookers to sell handguns and other so-called self-defense weapons for the fishermen in the weapons industry. In the United States, we are afraid of home invasion by the bogeyman, whoever or whatever that may be. This campaign of fear is pushed at us in the evening news and much of the entertainment we watch. From all manner of war movies to the video games we and our children play, we are inundated with the idea that violent behavior is normal. Violence is to be expected and we should have a plan to deal with it. We must do what we can to protect ourselves. Because of the fear pushed at us, we must constantly watch out for evil, lock our doors, and buy more guns.

It also must be noted that the fear of communists and communism has been subdued by the fact that the People's Republic of China has become more open to trade with the United States. The People's Republic of China is still a communist country. The fishermen, however, are there buying less expensive labor. The fishermen manufacture a large number of products in China that used to be manufactured here in the United States. The fishermen have slid away from making us fear an attack from the Chinese. They feel that we shouldn't be fearful of the Chinese communists because they are making huge profits in China, both as a marketplace for their goods and as a place to obtain low-cost labor. Our fishermen are truly internationalist.

This brings us to another of the baits that the fishermen use through their paid hookers: the politicians of the Republican Party Speaker of the House John Boehner said that voters in the 2010 election gave his party the majority in the House of Representatives for one reason and that was, "Jobs, jobs, jobs." His party has done nothing to actually stimulate job growth in the United States. The reality is to the contrary, in fact. Speaker Boehner and his band of far right wing hookers in Congress have done little but obstruct President Obama since they gained the majority in the House in the 2010 election. President Obama and the Democrats have made efforts to compromise with the right wing conservative hookers to get programs in place that would stimulate job growth in the United States. President Obama's efforts, as well as efforts put forth by other Democrats have been either ignored in the Republican-led House or filibustered in the senate. This is called obstructionism. It is what the Republican hookers have done since 2010. They have blocked every effort to create job growth and are now spending huge amounts of fishermen's money to make the fish believe that it is President Obama and the Democrats that aren't doing anything.

The Republican nominee for president has also been identified as a job outsourcer during his time at Bain Capital and during his time as governor of Massachusetts. But still, despite his record, former Governor Romney and Speaker Boehner continue to throw out the jobs, jobs, jobs bait. What is really amazing is that there are still fish going for this very wooden, artificial, overused, and chewed-up bait.

Another one of the baits that the fishermen use is smaller government. The fishermen say they want to get government out of the way of the job creators who are, they want us to believe, the "small" businessmen and women you might see on the main street in your community. They try to confuse the real small businessmen with the fishermen. The term "job creators" makes a much more enticing sound bite than "rich guys." This is a masterful use of language on the fishermen's part. This use of language is the bait. In reality, this bait conceals the hook of less regulation of the fishermen's business interests and the products and services they provide. Without government regulation, fishermen can and will do anything to create more profit. These fishermen will blow up the dam to get the fish in the reservoir. The fish won't know what happened until they are frying in the skillet. Without regulation, these fishermen will innovate less. They will be more deceptive with consumers. These deceptive tricks are already happening. You may have already noticed some of these tricks. Because of reduced retail regulation and the deceitful character of our fishermen in the food industry, things like changing the amount of product in what was a sixteen-ounce coffee container so that they look and cost the same but now contain only ten and a half ounces have become standard. In effect, consumers are paying the same price for less actual product. They will make a package that once was a half gallon (two quarts) of ice cream now contain only one and three-quarters quarts of ice cream but still sell for the same price as a half gallon. These things might sound small, but to our fishermen, they mean more of the holy of all holies, and that is *profit*. With less government our fisherman will have less regulation over the production of our food, housing, stock market, banking industry, water, air, and land. In effect, they will be given the permission to rape the public. When they have taken everything that is of any value whatsoever, they will move on and we, the citizens, will be left to clean up their mess.

The biggest and most effective bait is the abortion issue. Here, some of our fishermen and some of their hired gun hookers might have to get together with a few of their constituents. They might have to get into the water with them and pretend to be fish. What I am referring to here is that our fishermen and certainly their hookers might have to pretend to be Christians and maybe even occasionally, if not regularly, attend church with the fish they are trying to hook. But believe it or not they are not fish, just very cunning fishermen and hookers. Abortion, which is called "right-to-life" on the right and "pro-choice" on the left, is perhaps the most difficult moral issue of our time. The debate may never be resolved short of armed conflict. In fact, armed conflict is already happening in the extreme far-right Christian conservative crowd. The murder of Dr. James Tiller while he attended a church service is one example of this type of violence. There are those on the far right of Christian conservatism who are making it frightening and even dangerous to be in the female reproductive medical profession. These radical Christian conservatives stalk and persecute members of the professional medical community who are involved in any way with women's reproductive health. The issue is a mixture of religious beliefs and rights guaranteed by the United States Constitution and upheld by the Supreme Court. Mix those things with trying to determine the exact point at which a mixture of chemicals in a woman's body becomes a human being, and the debate rages. This intense debate may never be totally settled. The right-to-life bait is used to catch Christians. Christians hear it from the pulpits in their churches. What they don't seem to hear from these same pulpits is the fact that the so-called pro-life right wing conservative politician hookers are some of the most un-Christian people you will ever meet. They are the ones most likely to start wars and kill people. They are the same ones who are pro-gun. These hookers are the same ones who want to let poor children go hungry. They are the same ones who want these poor people to get jobs but don't want to fund public education and training so that they might find employment. They are the same ones who, a short time ago, were vehemently calling for the separation of church and state, which is in the US Constitution, and at the same time calling for the Christian belief that a marriage is between one man and one woman be made into law. This law, known as the Defense of Marriage Act, or DOMA, is being hotly debated in a Supreme Court that is divided down party lines. These same fishermen and hookers, who are trying to say that they want the government out of their businesses, are the same fishermen and hookers who are calling for the government to be deep in a woman's business just to bait and hook as many Christian votes as they possibly can. One of the Christian Ten Commandments is "Thou shall not bear false witness." Our fishermen and their hookers break this commandment with almost every word they utter.

THE FISHING LINE

In the past, fishing lines were made from a black string called catgut. Today these fishing lines are made from synthetic materials that are very narrow, very strong, and almost invisible in the water. When the fish don't see the line, they are less wary of taking the bait. It is the same with our fish and fishermen.

Just like our fishing line from the past, we had laws that made it much more likely that voters could see the money, or fishing line, and where it came from. But in today's world, post Citizens United decision, the money line is much more difficult, if not impossible, to see and follow.

Our right-biased Supreme Court has made corporations into people by giving them the same right to free speech as regular citizens. They have said that money is equal to speech and, since we have free speech, that any amount of money can be used to express ideas.

The next time you see a political television advertisement, check to see who paid for that advertisement. If it is negative and against any Democratic candidate or idea, it will probably show some real patriotic-sounding group in very small, oftentimes blurry lettering. You will have to be quick to see it because it will disappear quickly. It will say something like "Crossroads GPS" or "Freedom Foundation" or "The Club for Growth." These organizations are like the invisibility cloak for big-money donors in right wing politics today.

These organizations hide money given by our rich fishermen on the right side of our politics. They hide the donor identities but are able to push their ideas into the public's collective mind.

There are, of course, left-wing Political Action Committees, or PACs. The difference is in the number of donors and the average amount each donates. In fact, there are a much larger number of multi-million-dollar donors to right wing PACs than there are to left wing PACs. There are also many more individuals who donate to left leaning PACs but the donations are much smaller in size. These numbers add up to one conclusion. While donations are much larger on the right than the left, more individuals support the left. The information is available to those who choose to find it. As voters it is our duty to find the truth.

Why do these fishermen need to hide? Most of these really patriotic-sounding groups have donors that do not want to be known. These donors, our fishermen, usually have businesses that are in the public domain. That is, they sell products to the public. One such fisherman is Sheldon Adelson. He is a very wealthy businessman. He is in the casino business. He likes to donate but he keeps his donations quite secret, as his casino take might be negatively impacted if citizens knew what he used the money they lost in his casinos for. As mentioned earlier, the Koch brothers own a huge corporation that they call a small business because of the number of owners, although their corporation is in no other way small. Their "small" family business owns Kimberly-Clark. Kimberly-Clark is the huge lumber and paper company that retails Brawny paper towels and is just one part of their huge petrochemical conglomerate.

One of the reasons these fishermen want to hide is that it is far easier to sway the average voter into taking their bait if that voter cannot see who is baiting them. Hiding the money trail helps these fishermen keep from being caught. It is far easier to sell a tax cut if the people think it is only going to benefit the middle class, when in reality these tax cuts weaken the local governments' ability to provide infrastructure needed by the middle class. The rich fishermen benefit far more in real dollars and in the fact that they don't need the infrastructure. They have enough money to build roads and buy helicopters, planes, or jets, and build small airports to fly these in and out of. The fishermen don't need schools or teachers as they can hire them for their families. They don't need police or fire protection as they can provide and often do provide their own security forces. If one of their many homes catches fire, it can just be rebuilt with their own cash. They don't want social security, as they and theirs will always have more than enough cash. They don't need medical coverage. No medical bill will phase a person who can buy the hospital.

They can cover all these things and don't want to help the rest of us with ours. This might sound like a reasonable thing until we think about how and where these fishermen got their wealth. Most of them inherited substantial amounts of cash. Most of us probably contributed to the building of the fortunes they inherited either by working for their parents or by paying the profits on the things their families sold. Many of them say they worked hard and "made" their money. Saying they made the money is a stretch, as both you and I have known many citizens who have worked hard for a lifetime and may have amassed, at the most, several hundred thousand dollars. Some have accumulated more, but many more have struggled to obtain much less. The real answer to how they obtained their wealth is that most of them were extremely fortunate and had a lot of help. Some bent or outright broke laws in order to make their fortunes. Some worked hard to get laws changed to favor their own corporations at the peril of others around them. Some few were honest innovators. But in today's world, innovators have very little chance of developing their ideas. No matter how beneficial their innovations might be, our fishermen block innovators and/or steal the innovations in order to protect and ensure their own profits.

BOBBERS

In the real world, some fishermen use what is called a bobber. Bobbers are tied to the fishing line between the hook and the fishermen. They have two uses. One use is in the presentation of the bait. This use of a bobber sets the depth of the bait. The bobber floats on the surface and the hook is suspended at a certain depth below it. The other, better-known use of the bobber is as an indicator that a fish is biting the bait down in the water where the fisherman cannot see. If the bobber is pulled under, the fisherman knows a fish has taken his bait.

In the political world, the bobber would be the opinion polls and demographic studies that our fishermen study to see what effect their bait, such as TV, radio, print, and online advertising, is having on the hearts and minds of potential voters. If the poll numbers go up, the desired effect is taking place. If the poll numbers go down, then it might be time to adjust the bait.

Poll results have huge impacts on the number of fish our fishermen catch. You might hear a certain politician say that he or she does not look at the opinion polls. If you hear that from one of our hookers, you have almost surely just heard that hooker telling a lie. Hookers are known to do that on occasion.

MASTER BAITERS

In the real world, on a very large commercial or charter fishing vessel, there might be a deckhand that is very good at selecting and presenting the bait. This person selects the size of the hook and the shape and action of artificial lures that might be used. He might get input from the fishermen about what type of fish they want to catch. He also watches the bobber closely to see if his baiting techniques are working. He might suggest to the fishermen or captain that the vessel be moved to another location or that another type of bait be used. This truly important person might also be called a "master baiter."

In our analogy, the master baiters do very much the same things as the ones in the real world. These master baiters are *unelected*, hired professionals. They might be called political analysts, media specialists, communications directors, campaign coordinators, or any number of special-sounding titles. But in effect they are just master baiters. They look at data from opinion polls, or bobbers, and adjust the media formats in response to them. These master baiters also keep a watchful eye on things that the hookers are saying. More often in today's political world, the hookers won't say much without the approval of the master baiters.

One of the most famous of our master baiters is Karl Rove. Mr. Rove has been involved in right wing politics since the 1970s, and he has done some great baiting along the way. He once bugged his own office and blamed the bugging on a political opponent. This bit of deceit is just one example of the fact that he is willing to go to any length to hook voters.

Another of the right wing's master baiters is the master of master baiters, Rush Limbaugh. Mr. Limbaugh has been called a lot of things, from a bloviating buffoon and a right wing zealot to a brilliant leader of the conservative movement. He has a substantial following on right wing conservative talk radio. Make no mistake about it, though, he baits his audience by spewing right wing catch phrases, and he is a master at his master baiting craft.

Another person who makes the list of right wing master baiters is Glenn Beck. He was most notably known for his Fox "News" Channel program, *The Glenn Beck Show*. There is an ongoing debate as to the reason why Mr. Beck is no longer hosting his show on the Fox network. Some say his rhetoric got to the point that the Fox network's attempt to portray itself as "fair and balanced" was getting impossible to maintain because of Mr. Beck's daily, maniacal ranting about government conspiracies and the like. He now has his own right wing conservative radio talk show, where he continues his daily craziness. He maintains a substantial listening audience, which just goes to show that his master baiting seems to be working.

Next in this line of master baiters for the conservative right wing is Sean Hannity. Sean Hannity is a right wing conservative television host, talk radio personality, and author of three *New York Times* best-selling books.

Charles Krauthammer is also on our list of master baiters. He is an American Pulitzer Prize-winning syndicated columnist. He is known more for his writing and is also a contributor to Fox News.

Others on the master baiter list include Ann Coulter, Mike Huckabee, Michelle Malkin, George Will, David Brooks, Ross Douthat, Mike Gerson, and David Frum, to name just a few.

MINI BAITERS

In the real world of fishing, it is sometimes a practice to use live minnows as bait to catch other fish. It is a very effective way to fish. The minnows are used by hooking them through their backs and suspending them in the water for other fish to see. The minnows can survive like this for long periods of time. They are suspended in the water swimming, thinking they are free and living their lives. These little minnows don't even know they are no longer free. They don't realize they have become the bait.

So it is in our analogy of right wing politics. There are small fish that have been caught and then begin to take in the rhetoric of the right. They find themselves listening to right wing talk radio and reading books suggested by some master baiter on Fox News or some other form of extreme-right wing-bias media. If you go almost anywhere in a crowd of more than five people you will likely see one, but you will more likely hear them before you see them. They are the ones who talk a few decibels above everyone else. They usually don't listen. They often point when they argue their often almost silly-sounding points. They talk in a condescending voice and manner, as if what they are telling you is from the same mountain from which Moses is supposed to have brought the Ten Commandments. They often have very short hair or even shaved heads. These mini baiters will often wear high-top work boots even in the heat of the summer. They are more times than not in very good physical shape, which has been called having a "God bod." Their conversations—that is, their imposition of ideas—revolve around very few topics. One of their favorite topics is some kind of tax that they don't think is "fair." Another topic these mini baiters will talk about might be how Sharia law is being imposed on the United States. Sharia law is basically the use of the Muslim holy book, the Koran, to adjudicate civil justice. The first time I heard that one I had to grab my coat and leave, as I thought for sure the man had lost his mind. As I look back now, I think he had. This is part of the brainwashing of the gullible by right wing media. Another topic might be gun control and yet another would be, of course, the right-to-life/freedom-of-choice issue. I no longer try to argue with these mini baiters. Any one of these issues is usually of utmost importance to them. They have been fed lots of questionable information by right wing media and are usually more versed in that single topic. It is similar to an attorney walking into a trial without discovery. That is, you have not pondered the evidence and the facts of the case that these mini baiters have pondered and studied. Though a case could easily be made by someone well versed in the topic, even then these people will continue to drive home their ideas with stretched truths and bent or broken facts.

Like the minnow is to real-life fishermen, these mini baiters are just little minnows with hooks through their backs, presenting themselves as bait to try to catch other fish. Most, if not all, have absolutely no idea whatsoever that they are just bait being used ultimately by our fishermen to catch other fish, so that those fish can be used to catch other fish, and so on and so on.

The most disturbing aspect of these mini baiters, to this author, is the fact that some of them are people who should never have been hooked in the first place. I speak of members of labor unions. These people have taken one of our fishermen's baits, such as gun control, right-to-life, racial bias, tax issues, or any one of a large number of issues, and have been hooked on that single issue. These very mis-informed but well-hooked union brothers or sisters are now part of this growing force of mini baiters. I personally know people who have been fortunate enough to be under the umbrella of union-negotiated benefits their entire life and have now been hooked by a single issue. The horrible thing is that these mini baiters don't seem to realize that one of the main goals of our fishermen is to destroy any type of labor representation, public or private. When and if our fishermen, with the help of these mini baiters, cause this destruc-tion of labor unions, these very same mini baiters who are union members could lose many, if not all, of their hard-earned bene-fits. They will be hard pressed if not totally unable to find new employment or start new careers, especially in the difficult job market they would find themselves in today.

Many of the mini baiters are not from union work environments and would be much better off if they were, but they have been force-fed the evils of the union. There are admittedly things that are not perfect with labor unions. But I can think of nothing that would benefit workers more, and our country for that matter, than to have everyone who works become a union member of some kind. I have worked in both environments and, if nothing else, the union shops are much safer places to make a living. Wages and benefits of unionized workers are always better than those of nonunion workers. I have heard mini baiters argue that in the auto industry nonunion workers are paid as much as their union counterparts. If those nonunion workers are being paid the same they can and should thank their union brothers and sisters for that fact, since the United Auto Workers (UAW) negotiated for higher benefits in the union factories. They have set the standard. Believe me, if our fishermen complete their task of getting rid of unions, the wages and benefits in all nonunion workplaces will tumble. There will be no competition or standard. The nonunion shops will suffer just as much as the union shops will.

If you are in a situation where one of these mini baiters is trying to bait you or those around you, be very careful. Unless you are very well informed on the subject he or she is baiting you with, I would not engage him or her. The mini baiters have been brainwashed by the master baiters, or the professionals in the right wing media. Once these mini baiters have swallowed the hook, it seems that no one can change their minds. I have tried. I have seen very well-educated, well-informed, passionate, strong-minded people try with little success. I have seen these mini baiters boxed in and beaten with logic and truth, but they will not stop. I hate to say this, but these people act as if they were possessed by demons or have been turned into one-issue robots.

Watch out for the mini baiters near you. They might sound good, but they always have a well-hidden hook.

WHALERS

In the real world of fishing, the largest of all fish is the whale. We must realize, however, that a whale is not a fish but a mammal. A whale must come to the surface to breathe air. Whales also nurse their young, but they do live their lives entirely in the water and look and swim like fish. They are the largest living creatures on earth. They are caught by a certain group of fishermen called whalers. Whaling is done today from huge ships, with whalers getting as close to the whale as possible with the ship. The whalers wait until the whale comes up for air and then shoot a huge harpoon with a very large barbed, pointed tip into the whale. The whale bleeds to death and then is cut into pieces. The pieces are then rendered down to get the oil from the blubber of the whale.

In our analogy, the whale represents the Christian conservatives. This group of voters is huge and they are the only way right wing politicians can survive in today's political world. Remember, our fishermen are powerful because of the amount of money they have at their disposal, but they only have, in actuality, a few thousand votes. This makes it virtually impossible for them to elect anyone to political office unless they use their wealth to sway huge groups of voters. These citizen voters must be lead to believe that the politicians they are going to vote for are going to do things that are important to them.

The one and only thing our fishermen can offer for bait to this group is the right-to-life issue. With this single issue, our fishermen sway millions of Christians to believe that the right wing represents all that is good in American politics. Through the use of the First Amendment, which in part says that the government will make no law regarding religion, our fishermen, who are masters of baiting and slippery speak, have realized that the opposite is true: religious groups can be used to influence government. It is an extremely fine line we speak of here. The vast majority of Christians believe a women's choice not to carry a fertilized egg to full term is the murder of a child. There are those who believe, even in the Christian community, that a woman should have the right to decide whether or not to continue the pregnancy. It is one of the most difficult decisions a woman will ever have to make. There are many factors to consider when making this decision. One of these factors is the mother's ability to financially support the child. Other factors include the viability of the fetus. Also the ability of the woman to survive the pregnancy and birth must be considered.

Anyone who steps away from either side of this issue should easily be able to see the hypocrisy. Those who are calling for less government, less regulation, and less money for social welfare are the same who are calling for bills that would directly involve the government in a woman's decision to choose what she does with her own life and body.

This one issue has led many Christian people to be blinded and brainwashed. Their thinking is that because of the right wing's position against a women's right to chose, they should support all things right wing. The right wing believes in huge defense spending, no gun control, and less or, if possible, no help for people who are less advantaged. They have convinced the Christians through the use of this one issue that the right wing conservative plan of lower taxes for the wealthiest among us is a good thing while at the same time calling for less help for the poorest among us. These are not the teachings of Jesus Christ but are in fact the influences of our fishermen. Our fishermen's voices are small in number but huge in volume because of their wealth and can be heard from many pulpits in the church.

Our fishermen, in this case, have become whalers with this one issue. They have pulled their whaling vessel, the USS *Miss Information*, up alongside the Christian church and harpooned it like a big, fat, unknowing whale. The church is now bleeding in the water because of it. Our fishermen, who have become whalers, are smiling and saying, "This is good...for us."

WHOPPERS

In the real world of fishing, stories of huge fish are told about the ones that got away. These stories and the fish are often referred to as whoppers.

The whoppers are another large group of voters who have been swayed by right wing rhetoric to cast their ballots for hookers that will actually represent and work for our fishermen. This group actually might have a few of our fishermen as part of the members of their group.

Over the past century, farming in the United States has gone from what was once a highly labor-intensive, usually small family business to what it is today. Today, instead of two hundred acres as in 1900, a single farmer might own two thousand acres. In 1900 he may have needed a family of ten or more plus some extra help to take care of the farm. With the invention and expansion of the use of the internal combustion engine and the use of other farm implements, the need for all that labor has gone to nearly nothing. One single farmer today might farm two thousand of his own acres and lease at least that many acres from other landowners who choose to keep the land but not farm. Instead of needing twenty full-time farmhands, today's farmer might not need anyone other than himself to farm the vast acreages he plants and harvests. From the small family farm, today's farms and farmers have become farming corporations.

We must realize that today's farms and farmers are huge business operations. These farmers have GPS and laser guidance systems on million-dollar machines to maximize efficiency and profits. As with other businesses, these farmers are willing to work as hard in the political field as they do in the farm fields. Regulations and taxes are today's farmers' biggest concern. Farmers in the past were concerned about the weather, insects, and the price of their produce. Today's farmers are more concerned about the cost of irrigation, futures markets, insecticide regulations, genetic modifications of food crops, and of course taxes. Today's farmers hate taxes but they love their government crop subsidies.

Farmers are part of a larger problem, which is the industrial food supply system in the United States and, for that matter, the world. This topic is large enough to encompass an entire library of written work. For this analogy, let us say that farming today is part of this huge industrial operation. Farmers have been swayed by the owners of this operation. Some of today's farmers are, in fact, big enough to be part owners of this industrial-type food supply system. Since some of our farmers are what we are calling fishermen, we will call these farmers "Whoppers." Our Whoppers do not like the government even though they get huge subsidies from the government. They do not like taxes, but the taxes they pay come back to them in the form of higher food sales. Our Whoppers don't like the people who are on supplemental nutrition assistance programs (SNAP). SNAP is a group of programs that people once referred to as food stamps or welfare. The food that is bought with SNAP funds, however, is almost always helping farmers and the industrial food supply as much as it does the people using SNAP.

It is difficult to understand why farmers, who are usually a very well-informed group, don't like SNAP even though they almost directly and certainly indirectly benefit from the program. But if we go back to the Christian conservative chapter called "Whalers" and realize that most of the farmers in the United States are, in fact, Christians, it becomes a little easier to understand. Whoppers and whalers are generally both Christian conservatives. Our Whoppers, who are also our whalers, are blinded and brainwashed from the pulpits of their churches to blindly follow whatever the political right says in order to put an end to a woman's choice about what she should do with her body and life.

FISHING POLES AND BROAD CASTERS

On a real fishing boat, the one thing that almost all boats have is at least one good fishing pole. A fishing pole is used along with a reel full of fishing line to cast the bait far out into the water. The idea is to get the bait as far away from the fishing boat as possible. Fish are easily frightened, and the farther a fisherman can cast the bait from the boat, the less likely the fish are to be frightened and the more likely they are to take the bait and be hooked. The fishing poles are also used to haul the fish back into the boat. Fishing poles can be used over and over again. They can use different baits and lines. There are also different types of poles and reels, depending on the fish that are being baited.

In our analogy, the fishing pole represents the different types of right wing media. Television is one of the most effective ways our fishermen bait the voting public. The voters might otherwise find that these politicians are not going to do any good for them. Broadcasters of right wing television have their viewers so convinced that other news networks are biased or deceptive that these viewers neither seek nor get any other political information. It might be said that left wing media uses the same tactics. As a regular viewer of left wing media, I can say that they do not proclaim to be "fair and balanced." Left wing media admits it is giving the opposing view. It usually also admits when it has made factually incorrect statements. I have never heard or seen left leaning media say not to view right leaning media. They do spend a lot of time correcting incorrect information being broadcast by right wing broadcasters. On the other hand, right wing broadcasters have convinced their viewers that this one-sided, right-biased view is balanced and fair. In the mainstream media (which are sometimes referred to as the "lame stream media" by those on the right), especially around election time, the right wing super PACs with huge amounts of money from our fishermen use negative advertising to bait those who don't follow the right wing so-called news. Many times through this mainstream media and negative television advertising, our fishermen can destroy the reputation of an opposing political figure by blasting the airwaves with negative and very often misleading, if not outright false, information. Since the Supreme Court decision in the Citizens United case, advertisers are no longer required by federal election laws to reveal who is paying for this advertising as long as it does not directly support a candidate. Even if the negative advertising pushes the limits of factuality and shoots holes in the reputation of a candidate, the advertising is allowed as long as it can be said to be issue-based and not for any given candidate. This is what the Swift Boaters for Truth campaign did to John Kerry's military service reputation. This Swift Boater campaign used paid-for misinformation that had a measurable impact on the outcome of that election. And that was before the Supreme Court's Citizens United decision.

Our fishermen rely heavily on right wing talk radio, also. Not long ago, if you traveled across the vast rural areas of our great country and turned on the radio, you would have found that the only stations available in many places were right wing or Christian conservative talk radio. They had a captive, bored audience. With the advent and use of more satellite radio, this is less true now than it was even ten years ago, but the base audience has been established and these programs are even more directed toward a less and less well-informed group of listeners. Also, these right wing radio and television broadcasters are relying on the measurable decline in the amount of political information that Americans, in general, spend time taking in. The broadcasters know that most people have become much more inclined to view programming that entertains more than it informs. Generally, Americans are much more inclined to view shows like *American Idol*, *Dancing with the Stars*, or *Monday Night Football* than a presidential debate. When it comes to being informed about national, congressional, state, and local politics, the American viewer becomes completely turned off and would rather spend his or her time being entertained than informing himself or herself about real-world politics. It is a shame for our democracy, but it is what it is and right wing broadcasters have aggressively taken advantage of this desire to be entertained rather than informed.

FISHERMEN'S ONLY
X-CHANGE

In the real world of fishing, most of today's boats have radios, a global positioning system (GPS), and radar. Lots of fishermen are talking on the marine channels to get information about where the fish are and who is catching what and how. Some fishermen are what might be called unscrupulous or even downright dishonest. These fishermen will provide misinformation in order to conceal the real information about their fishing effectiveness.

In our analogy, the same is true if not truer than real life. We could say that the USS *Miss Information* has a twenty-four hours a day, seven days a week, fifty-two weeks a year broadcast outlet that tells the other fishermen and the general public that the news they broadcast is real and believable. They tell their listeners that the information that is broadcast from the shore (mainstream or "lamestream" media) is untrue or biased to the left. This broadcast outlet might be called the Fishermen's Only X-Change (FOX) News. "News" is a stretch. It is, in fact, a purposefully misleading or misinformation network. Roger Ailes proposed the concept of FOX to President Richard M. Nixon during the Nixon administration. Basically, Mr. Ailes proposed a national TV outlet from which the right wing's point of view could be broadcast. Roger Ailes now runs the FOX News channel. "Fair and balanced" is their description of what their programming is supposed to be. It is definitely not fair or balanced. It is, in fact, exactly what Mr. Ailes proposed to Richard Nixon, and that is a right wing information outlet. Many call it a right wing propaganda outlet.

Now we must go back to our fishing analogy. In the real world, fishermen with radios on their boats might come across a school of big ones that are hungry for their bait. The other fishermen in the area can see with binoculars that there is activity on the other fishermen's boat but can't see well enough to tell what type of bait is being used, the depth at which they are fishing, and other particulars of the successful fishermen. The fishermen then get on the radio and ask the other fishermen what the particulars are. The successful fisherman might call back saying that he is using the same bait they used yesterday. The implication is thought to be clear, having told the other fishermen the night before in the local fishermen's tavern that they had used blue artificial bait. What they do not tell them is the fact that they also used a yellow bait, which they didn't bring up the night before. This use of omission is a simple but effective way that the Fishermen's Only X-change can use to put out information that is not completely true but not completely false either. They use this, among many misinformation tactics like it, to deceive their audience.

OILERS AND ENGINEERS

In the real world, if a fishing boat is big enough, the owners hire a group of people who are responsible for keeping the ship running as part of their crew. These people are called marine engineers. They are constantly going around the ship oiling and greasing things to make sure things are moving easily. Sometimes they are called oilers.

On the USS *Miss Information*, "oilers" who go around and make sure things are oiled and greased are the lobbyists. Lobbyists are people who represent the people who pay their salaries. The lobbyists usually work for groups with the funding needed to provide the necessary perks to gain access to elected officials. Sometimes they represent groups like labor unions or a local community group. More often than not though, lobbyists represent huge, corporate, moneyed interests. These interests include the oil and chemical industry, lumber, mining, construction, and pharmaceuticals, and the list goes on and on. Virtually every person or group of people who can afford to pay can get themselves an oiler to gain access to any political figure. On the USS *Miss Information* the people paying the oilers would be our fishermen. Our oilers go around Washington, DC, making sure that the ideas of the people they represent are put into or taken out of legislation before Congress. These oilers can also be a beneficial link between large groups of people and their nationally elected representatives. These large groups of people often pool their resources in order to hire a lobbyist. If not for these lobbyists, it would be difficult if not virtually impossible for any single member or even a representative group of these large groups of people to individually talk with members of Congress. But oilers can also be a way for a few or even a single very wealthy individual, one of our fishermen for example, to change the balance of power.

The ways our oilers may get access to representatives are varied. One way is to host a fundraiser to help a certain member of Congress raise money for reelection campaigns. There are all manner of ways our oilers might get access to these representatives. The line goes right up to and often crosses into outright bribery.

DAM FISHERMEN

In the real world of fishing, fishermen often fish in rivers or creeks that once flowed freely but are now being held back by dams. The dammed water builds up to form lakes known as reservoirs. Depending on the size of the river, the size of the dam, and the lay of the land behind these dams, the lake can be anywhere from a small pond to a huge, deep lake. These dams can change the habitats for certain species of native fish and, in some cases, force some of them into extinction. Often introduced into these reservoirs are fish species that are not native to the original river but can thrive in the calmer, slower flowing water of the reservoir. Fishermen in the real world find these reservoirs very attractive.

In the natural world, some dams are built by beavers. A very few of the smaller, man-made dams are built with private funds. The land and water behind these smaller dams, if built on privately owned land with private funds, become the private property of the people who built the dams. The larger dams are always built with the assistance of public funds. The largest dams are built completely with public funds, since these undertakings are too massive even for the wealthiest. To be clear, the reader should understand that "public funds" means money collected from the larger community by some sort of government body. These community funds are usually collected through some sort of tax or fee. These larger communities may be local, state, and national governments. Fishing and other activities in the publicly funded reservoirs are usually controlled by laws passed by the public entity whose funds built the dam. Maintenance of the dams should also be provided by the owner, whether public or private.

The reservoir in this analogy represents the democratically governed place we call the United States of America. It also represents the various smaller entities of government. These government entities have written constitutions and laws that not only ensure that we are free to pursue happiness, but also to provide a structure of rules that guarantees we *all* have the right to equal treatment under these laws. This in no way means that we are all equal. Our Constitution only guarantees that we as citizens should be treated equally under the law. Some of our fishermen, however, think that because they are wealthy almost beyond our ability to comprehend, they are not subject to the same set of laws that govern the rest of us. With that in mind, they are using their wealth to influence the outcome of elections. These controlled elections are putting in place politicians who represent our fishermen's desires for less government regulation and also more profit on their bottom lines simply by cutting our fishermen's taxes. This is evident through the use of the movement the fishermen have started called the Tea Party. Many of the people in this movement think it is a grassroots organization. It is clearly not a grassroots effort. The Tea Party movement was started by and funded by money from our fishermen. Anyone who thinks otherwise is simply deceiving himself or herself. The proof is hard to find and often subtle, but it can be found. Our fishermen provide free bus transportation, professionally printed protest signs, venues that might otherwise be restricted from public protest, and many forms of not-so-grassroots help.

Our dam could also represent the infrastructure that holds our very society together. Our huge, mighty dam was built with the labor of many workers. The capital of the wealthy, as well as tax money collected from those of more modest means, has built the dam that has allowed our reservoir to become what it is. It has been a partnership. Our fishermen seem to have forgotten that it was this partnership that helped make them what they have become. Our fishermen are out on the reservoir with their huge boat, the USS *Miss Information*, trying to get things changed so that they can be the only boat on the water. When that happens, they will be the only ones fishing. At that point they will no longer need the fish. Our fishermen might decide they no longer want or need to fish for votes and will just change the laws about fishing. They are already moving in that direction. Our fishermen are currently trying to rid the reservoir of labor unions, both public and private. When this is done, our fishermen will have no real competition for the fish. At that time they may even decide to do what they have subtly been suggesting, which is to blow up the dam and start over.

FISH

In the real world of fishing, some fish are smarter than others. By this I mean that some fish are harder to catch. For this work we will only consider freshwater fish, since this is basically about fishing in the dam-built lake of the United States. One of the hardest fish to catch is the brook trout. They have a very specific diet that varies with the time of year and the climate. They can be caught with a method of fishing that is called fly fishing. The fishermen must first find out what bug is currently in the fish's environment. It might be mayflies or their larvae, or it could be mosquito larvae or whatever critter the fish finds naturally in its environment. The fishermen then tie an artificial fly that, when presented to the trout, resembles the bug that the fish is feeding on at that time. Even using this fly fishing technique, it's difficult to catch the brook trout since it lives in water that is normally cold and clear, and the brook trout has very good eyesight. Other fish in the real world are not as difficult to catch. Fish at the easier to catch end of the fish IQ scale might include the carp or bullhead. These fish usually live in the murky water at or near the bottom. These fish feed on almost anything with a strong smell that settles to the bottom.

Our fishermen go for the fish that are the easiest to catch. These include fish with less education and knowledge. These fish are usually rural people who have born-again Christian upbringings. They are people from the Bible belt. These voters work hard, save their money, and go to church almost every Sunday morning, often Sunday evening, and the ladies of these families might regularly attend Wednesday prayer meeting services. Christian churches are a central part of these people's lives. These are good people. Their Christian beliefs and goodness, however, have been and are being used by our fishermen to catch them. These good people's votes are being hooked by using what, to them, is irresistible bait: the right-to-life issue. Right-to-life or freedom-of-choice is the most divisive issue of our time. Our fishermen are taking full advantage of this issue.

Our fishermen hook a huge swath of voters by supporting the right-to-life issue. Our fishermen generally don't care about whether a woman goes full term with a pregnancy or not. Actually, I think that our fishermen would like to see poorer women have no children at all. They see these poor people's children as a potential burden to be taken care of by the taxes of the more affluent. The hypocrisy in this issue becomes clear if one takes a look at the legislation being proposed and supported by those hookers that our fishermen get elected. They vote regularly for legislation to end a woman's right to choose, and often on the same day they vote to cut assistance to help these same poor women feed the children that they literally forced into the world. It is a gut-wrenching decision for a woman to make, one way or the other. But the government should have no part in that decision, especially a government that wants to turn its back on these women and children once brought into this world.

Our fishermen hook another huge swath of fish with the right to bear arms argument by saying that the people on the left want to take away our citizens' right to bear arms. Our fishermen from the National Rifle Association (NRA) propose and push this idea. The arms industry in the United States is a huge mega business. Our fishermen from the NRA are lead by actor Charlton Heston. It is a known fact that a good actor makes a great salesman. The NRA and the right wing in general know this well. Ronald Reagan was a good actor that was used by our fishermen as one of the greatest salesmen in history for the right wing conservative movement. He was not a great or even a good leader. Ronald Reagan and Charlton Heston are tools being used by the same group of fishermen with regard to gun rights.

FISHING FROM THE BEACH

In real life there are those who go to the beach with the intention of fishing but never get to it. There is just too much other stuff on the beach to do. They might get involved in a beach volleyball game. There might be hot dogs cooking or watermelon cut and ready to snack on. There might be a cold beverage and a hot sun to enjoy. There are dozens of reasons not to put forth the effort to fish and to stay on the beach instead. Good weather, bad weather, or some people just don't like to fish.

So it is in our analogy. Our fishermen know the importance of catching fish and putting them in the boat. But just like the people on the beach, many voters just stay on the sidelines. They say it is not worth the effort to vote. They have been convinced that all politicians are the same. This is in itself a political tactic. Since the fishermen have the same number of votes per person as everyone else and there are far fewer of them, one of the easiest things the fishermen can do to sway elections is to get normal people who oppose their candidates or proposals not to vote. If the fishermen can convince a substantial portion of the electorate simply to stay home and not vote, it means that they have to persuade that many fewer voters to vote for their proposals and/or candidates. For them there is only one thing better than a vote for their side and that is an uncast vote that would have been cast for the other side. This principle was used in the election of 2012. Through the use of requirements for very specific voter identification, right wing state governors and legislatures forced people—mostly the poor, elderly, and those of color who would have most likely voted against them—to obtain these very specific forms of identification in order to vote. The justification for these new laws was to stop virtually non-existent voter fraud. In reality, these laws passed by the right are in fact voter suppression laws. It has been estimated that these new laws will affect as many as one million voters in the swing state of Pennsylvania alone. If only ten percent of these voters were unable to vote because of these new, unnecessary laws they could very well have swung the national election outcome. What a horrible thing for our democratic system that is.

Certainly a single vote will not sway a major election. A single vote might not even sway a local election. We have all heard this said by many of those single voters. The key word here is "many." When a single vote becomes many votes, the next step is that these many votes become enough votes. Many politicians know this well and even Mike Huckabee, the Republican former minister and once governor of Arkansas, has said publically that "If you know your neighbor is going to vote for the other guys, do what you can to make sure he does not vote, even if you have to let the air out of his tires."

FISH SANDWICH

In real life, when fishermen are done fishing and have caught all the fish they can for the day, they will go home and enjoy a nice meal. That dinner might be a piece of fried fish between two pieces of bread. It is a quick and easy meal for tired fishermen.

In our world of political fishermen, it is much the same as in the real world. In United States politics, there is a group of voters in the middle who are easy to catch and fry. They are the ones who, after the bases on both sides have decided for whom they will vote, actually make the real difference in most elections, especially the close ones. This fact is a very disheartening thing for those on the left who have worked and campaigned to elect people who will best represent the interests of most average middle class people. It is, on the other hand, a delightful thing for those on the right. The fishermen and their hookers know that with some last minute, very negative, often misleading advertising, gladly paid for with dollars from the fishermen, this group of poorly informed middle class voters can be easily swayed to their side. This small group of relatively uninformed voters is swinging the outcomes of more and more elections, from local through national.

The USS *Miss Information* is put to work here big time. The big right wing boat driven by the fishermen simply throws out several tens of millions of dollars to and through conservative PACs and catch the fish with a big net dragging behind their boat. Those in the middle six percent of the electorate, who are mostly uninterested, often uninformed fish, are taken in by the right wing negative advertising net that is paid for by the fishermen.

It would be great for our democracy if this most important voting group in the middle of the voting "fish sandwich" would somehow magically become aware of their importance to the outcome of elections. If they knew, perhaps they would take the time to be more informed instead of being misled by a few less-than-factual negative ads paid for by the fishermen. This important middle fish sandwich might realize that the fishermen do not have the average citizen's best interest in mind when they dump the multi-million-dollar donations into right wing PACs and politicians' campaign funds.

The fish in the middle of the fish sandwich are more than likely the swing votes that elected George W. Bush, who some people, including this author, believe was the worst president in American history. A Supreme Court, which was stacked with right-leaning justices, declared him the winner after an election that was too close to call. This exemplifies the importance of this undecided group of the electorate. If this narrow band of voters had taken the time to be more informed about how well our economy was doing under President Clinton's administration instead of being swayed by negative advertising paid for by the fishermen, our history could be completely different. Perhaps if Al Gore had been elected, he would have acted on information from the CIA about the terrorist group that Osama Bin Laden was assembling. Perhaps the terrorist act on 9/11 could have been thwarted. The United States could be leading the world in green energy development and education instead of falling further and further behind. Maybe, if this fish sandwich of voters had not been so easily swayed, we would not be spending more on defense than the next fifteen countries combined. Perhaps, if this very important fish sandwich would spend less time being entertained and more time on being informed, we would have a much stronger democracy.

PERSPECTIVES

In the real world, a fisherman knows a trout is not a catfish and a shark is not a tuna. They know this for two reasons. One reason is they have been taught by people they can trust what the different characteristics of each of these fish are. The other reason is because trout are not catfish and a carp is not a tuna. They are all fish, but they are not the same.

For the best illustration of how an individual or group of individuals' perspectives can be influenced, I will use a more common analogy since more people know about the difference between an apple and a pear.

Let us suppose that you are a young farmer who has lived his entire life in a very rural and isolated community. On your family farm you raise pears. Let us say, however, that you have been told throughout your life by your friends and family that pears are apples. Suppose your family always sells these "apples" in the closest town and that those people know you, and when you say you have come to town to sell your apples, the people in the town know that you mean pears. They never question the fact that you call your pears, apples. This has gone on for years, perhaps even generations. It gets to the point where the people in town start to believe that pears are apples. They are similar, and that is all they have ever heard a pear called. Let us say that one year a horrible rainstorm comes through your remote area and washes out the only bridge to the little town where you and your family sell your pears. It is harvest time. The pears are ripe and ready. You must get them to market but you can't get to town, so you decide you must go to the town in the other direction that is much further away. You harvest your "apples," load them in your wagon, cover them for protection, and away you go.

After a long journey you get to the new town. It is much bigger and has connections to the outside world. It has a train line and a telegraph. All the people in this town know the difference between pears and apples. You ask a person there how to get to the local farmers' market. You tell the person that in your wagon you have some fine apples for sale. The person gives you directions to the local market but also tells you that he has just come from the farmers' market. The person tells you that the man in charge of the farmers' market has too many apple farmers there and they are turning away farmers selling apples. You know the person is telling the truth, but you go to the farmers' market anyway. The person in charge of the farmers' market tells you exactly what the first person told you. He even says to you that if you had pears, he would love to have you sell them in his market. But since you don't know what pears are and your pride won't let you tell the man that you don't know what a pear is, you thank the man and leave. Since you are sure you have apples, you go back with your wagon of pears instead of what could have been the proceeds of a bountiful harvest. You and your family suffer through an unnecessarily long, hard winter because, from your perspective, you tried to sell apples that, from other people's perspective, were in fact pears.

This analogy simply illustrates that what a person is told to be true may not always be true, even if people we feel we can trust tell us those things. Those people may have been misinformed. There are also people in the political world who have agendas of their own that may not include your best interests, but they need your vote. It is extremely important that we question ideas that are presented to us. We must ask ourselves if the person presenting the information has a motive or reason to tell us things that might not be true. In addition to information from people, we can get information from other sources we think we can trust. It is always best to get information from more than one source. It is best to look at things from more than one point of view. If the honest person who ran the farmers' market in the apple/pear story had simply looked under the farmer's cover and seen that the "apples" were actually pears, both parties could have benefited.

It is critically important to get information from as many sources as possible in today's political world. It is critical that we ask questions. We must get as much information as possible. When we get that information, we must consider the perspective and the agenda of the people who gave us that information. We must also try to untangle the fishing line, or follow the money, as best we can. There are billionaires, fishermen, on the right that have been pursuing agendas for thirty years or more that are destructive to our democracy. Their agendas are bad for our democracy but great for the fishermen's own bottom lines. But please, don't take this author's perspective alone. I encourage you to get the perspective of others. Please get the most information from as many sources as possible and then think about what is best for you and yours. Then use your rights that our patriots are paying for every day with their blood and service. Use the knowledge that is your right and most of all, *vote*.

CONCLUSION—THE EPIC STRUGGLE

The United States is currently in an epic struggle. The participants are the few who have massive amounts of wealth and, on the other side of this struggle, the rest of us. To understand this struggle we must learn and keep in mind these few definitions:

Oligarchy: A form of government in which ruling power is in the hands of a few.

Plutocracy: A form of government by the wealthy; also a group of wealthy people who control or influence the government.

Democracy: A form of government where the people hold the ruling power either directly or through elected representatives; rule by the ruled.

In this work we have been most concerned with the ideas of oligarchy and plutocracy. The struggle with which we should all be concerned involves the attempts by a few with massive amounts of wealth to change our form of government from a democracy to a plutocracy. The shift is becoming more evident with each passing election cycle. The wealthy are not using guns and physical power—yet. That day may come sooner, regrettably, than we might think. The shift will happen and soon if our people—our average, you-and-me citizens—continue to focus more on our leisure and entertainment than we do on what is happening to our government. The potential plutocrats are using stealth as well as wealth to gradually ease themselves into power. The use of entertainment is a diversion like those used in a magic show. They might take the power of our government by subtle stages and misinformation, but once they have it they will do all they can to hold that power. As for now, the epic struggle is being done with ideas that stretch the truth and shape and bend the facts. It is being done with the use of language that has double meanings, much like the titles of the chapters of this work. Phrases like "job creators" have been wedged into people's minds. The phrase "job creators" is being used to make citizens think that these people with wealth and power want to create jobs, but in fact their only real concern is to create profits and even more wealth and power for themselves.

The most difficult question is not how or even if these plutocrats are trying to change our form of government. The difficult question is, "Why are they doing it?" To answer that is another story. For now, we as regular citizens and those in the upper middle class should only be concerned with the fact that it is being done, and only we can put an end to it. It will not be easy, for already huge swaths of our population have been made drunk with misinformation. These huge groups of voters have basically been brainwashed. They believe the plutocrats' extremely well-crafted magic show of deception and see it as real. These groups include the Christian conservatives, members of the National Rifle Association, and others. The plutocrats desperately need these and other huge groups of citizen voters to complete their takeover. The plutocrats only number in the tens of thousands if we include their extended families and closest associates. Tens of thousands of votes compared to hundreds of millions of votes just won't get it done. They certainly do not have the votes to change our system of government. They do, however, have the power of money. That power is being expressed in the form of television advertising on major networks, especially around election time. They have also had, since 1998, a twenty-four hour a day right wing propaganda outlet in the form of the Fox News channel. If you think it is anything other than right wing propaganda you are not alone. You have plenty of company. But the fact that you and others are being misinformed does not make you any more correct. It only means that you are captured pawns in this epic struggle. Escape from your mental prison is extremely difficult but possible. It will surely not be made easy by the plutocrats who have captured your mind and continue to give you misinformation. Only you can set yourself free. As we all know, "Freedom is not free."